WHISPERS OF MY HEART

WHISPERS

of
My Heart

— Regina Johnson —

PALMETTO

PUBLISHING

Charleston, SC

www.PalmettoPublishing.com

Copyright © 2023 by Regina Johnson

All rights reserved

Hardcover ISBN: 979-8-8229-3269-2

Paperback ISBN: 979-8-8229-3270-8

eBook ISBN: 979-8-8229-3271-5

ACKNOWLEDGEMENTS

Above all, I thank God for giving me the desire to share many of my storms, trials, hopes and joys as a history book of poetry to remind me of how far I have traveled through my personal journey. I am very happy to finally be sharing this book with others. Hopefully, it will be a blessing and inspiration to those who read it and can relate to it.

Many thanks to all who were involved in contributing to this project. I am sincerely grateful to everyone who simply believed in me, encouraged me, and graciously planted seeds of nurturing focus when I kept getting distracted from the process. You know who you are.

*Credit to SLO for giving me the following two poems as gifts to complement the history included in this project:

-Like God Wants Us to Be
-Wishing For You, My Friend

TABLE OF CONTENTS

I'LL BE THERE

I understand your race
And dedication to your goal
The struggle you face now
Will change as you unfold

And how you will unfold
Whether you fall or stand
Is determined by decisions
That must be made by a "man"

So honey, I will be there
To support you endlessly
Because the race, dedication and struggle
Are for us—your family.

NOW YOU'VE FOUND FOREVER
(My Daddy's Homecoming, 11.25.1997)

For now you've found forever
Struggles and pain are no more
True happiness is awaiting
Your heart shall sing and soar.

For now you've found forever
We'll treasure the times we've had
You have reached the ultimate destiny
No more reasons to be sad.

For now you've found forever
A place you've never been
But someday we all will meet you
Where JOY shall never end
AMEN.

MY FAMILY TREASURES

Thank you, Oh Lord
For my family
I love them so much
They're so dear to me

My husband and daughter
And also my son
You have blessed me with
Oh, Gracious One

This precious time
We have together
I give you the praise
For my priceless treasure

So these gifts I'll cherish
And love and adore
Until you will have us
Upon earth no more

And please Mighty God
When this life is done
We'll be with you
In your Heavenly Home!

THE GIFT

My greatest expression of love
Is within you everyday
It has little to do with words
But my heart stands up to say—
I've given a gift of myself
Hoping you have understood
The sacrifice I have made
Giving you the gift of fatherhood.

DON'T LOSE YOUR SPIRIT

Don't lose your spirit
It is the foundation
To the life you lead.
When the spirit is gone or stolen
You surely are dead.
Even though you still breathe
And walk among the living—
What is silent living
When you have no joy?
No joy means no laughter
No laughter means no light—
The light to your soul.
When your spirit is stolen
It means two things:
You must fight to restore the light,
Or blow it out and start anew.

AS I AM

I HAVE TO FEEL IT
SO DON'T COAX ME

I HAVE TO BELIEVE IT
SO DON'T BLAME ME

I HAVE TO BE INTO IT
SO DON'T FORCE ME

JUST LOVE ME
AS I AM—
BUT DON'T HURT ME.

"LAST MOMENTS WITH MOM"

Just saw you the other day
You appeared somewhat lost
Unusually just you and me
In that cold room that day.
I tried to make conversation
But you wouldn't utter a word
Unusually just you and me
In that cold room that day.
The television was your focus
No apparent awareness of my presence
Unusually just you and me
In that cold room that day.
Then I waved my hand
Through my eyes you saw your soul
Unusually just you and me
In that cold room that day.
My Daddy had shown me the sign
I told my Mother that I loved her
She found her place of rest
A year ago this day.
(9.17.2001)

(AKA DEPRESSION)

Known by so many names
Your design is quite unclear
I will not accept your control
Or surrender myself in fear.

Your desire seeks the weakened
Anxiety takes its place
I will not live in captivity
I'll retreat and win the race.

Your attitude dark and deadly
Your king is that of the night
I will not become your child
Or fall into the pit of fright.

I'll defeat your ugly plague
--Must destroy your heart of cold
I challenge your own misery
For my joy I will unfold.

LIKE GOD WANTS US TO BE

I will not bond to you
Through hatred, anger or resentment
I will do the things he intends me to do
For you I prayed, God answered and sent.

I will not drag myself in the darker worlds
Because there I cannot see
Again please, be my diamonds & pearls
Forgiving myself, I have released me.

There are long days and sleepless nights
When you're not here to hug
Let's continue to grow towards the goods and rights
So that God can nurture our love.

Never before have I realized the importance
Of my wife, children, the family
Let's build the trust to close the distance
So that we could be happy <u>LIKE GOD WANTS US TO BE.</u>

By: SLO

WISHING FOR YOU, MY FRIEND

We're still alive
We will survive
This moment of harsh
And pain

Let's start all over
With a four-leaf clover
Everything is a plus
To gain

At times it seems a demise
Our limit is the skies
For the flowers are beautiful
And yellow

Reach for my hand
Here I will stand
Trust my patience
And I will be mellow

My intent is not to offend
So please don't defend
My heart as I pour
It out

My love your love
Let the light shine from above
And it will grow
Without a doubt

I prayed from my heart
For you to be a part
And God truly
Did send

I do know however
Not trying to be clever
I'm wishing for you
My friend

By: SLO

NEW BEGINNINGS
(A new level of Hope)

H-humility & honesty
O-optimism & opportunity
P-pursuit & passion
E-energy & expectation

A CRY FOR WISDOM

I cried for wisdom
She came to me
She said, "Be patient
And seek eternity,
Be a blessing to others
As you grow in the Word
Invite them to the kingdom
Make sure you are heard;
Then all your desires
Will be given to you
For obedience is the way
To make dreams come true!"

DISTRESSED

Remove the spirit of sadness, pain, anxiety, depression...all that is not of God. I rebuke these spirits in the name of my Lord and Savior, Jesus Christ!

I invite your peace, comfort, and strength into my life right now, Heavenly Father. Make me whole again and trade my sorrows for your love and joy.

BE FREE!

Unclutter your closet!
Free yourself from undue pain
Discover and elevate the real woman
That God has designed you to be
And BE FREE!
Invite peace into your life;
Into your world.

WHAT IS LOVE?

Emotions and feelings
How they come and go
Unstable like the wind;
This one, that one,
Inconsistent end.
But true love is God—
Amazingly constant and strong
Balanced and perpetual
No blame or wrong;
GOD is LOVE.

GRIEVING A FRIEND

Finding a special friend
Is like finding true love
(They go together)
It may only come once
In a lifetime,
A second chance for few.
So value that relationship
Keep it polished and fresh
Nurture and encourage it
Accept it as it is
And love it for all its worth.
Spend time with it
And trust it completely—
Let doubt nor fear betray it
Don't take it for granted
Or ask it to change
Lest it roams elsewhere.

BE MINDFUL

We can NEVER exhale
While on this earth;
For if we do
We allow the enemy
To have leverage
Upon our thoughts, our words,
Our actions and our lives.
We must always
Inhale and absorb
The sweet spirit of Jesus
Until we have returned
To dust.

THE VOICE OF TRUTH

The voice of truth
Is just that—
It does not waver
Is not confused
But is absolutely
Exact in completeness.
We must be open
To receive it
So that we
Can hear it.
Sometimes it whispers
We ignore or question it;
Sometimes it nags
We choose to flee from it;
Sometimes it must
SHOUT!!!!!!!
Before we give attention
To its validity and power;
Oh, Father God!
Pardon my excuses
Restore my desire
For your best—
For your truth
Is perfect always;
No matter what range, depth or pitch
It remains pure!

THE MEANING OF SUFFERING

Unless one stands naked before God
Stripped of pride, confidence, earthly resources
And the image of self,
He cannot see the meaning of suffering.
This perspective becomes clear
When helplessness and hopelessness
Are all that there is...
Or so it seems.
Calling upon the name of the Lord
Becomes our defense from
Darkness, pain, broken heartedness, faithlessness,
And an array of miseries that the spirit of affliction brings.
But suffering brings with it
The gift of humility;
It invites the presence of God and His Holy Spirit
Into our lives
It brings us closer to Him and Him to us
So He can lift us up!
Suffering is permitted to
Promote, enrich, and enhance
Our Christian and personal character.
Without it, we would never see
Ourselves for what we truly are;
Our learning, growth and the purpose
Of our journey would expire.

A POEM OF PRAYER

Dear Father God in Heaven
Thank you that you are the source
Of everything good in my life,
And the resource I seek
When I am weak.
I thank you for waking me this morning
Providing me with new
Mercies, grace, love, and opportunities
To praise you and know you more fully.
I invite you and your Holy Spirit
Into my life right now
To lead, direct, and guide
My words, thoughts, and actions this day.
May your order in my life
Be a model and blessing to others.
Please remove anything in me
That is not of you.
Protect me from the attacks of the enemy.
Please fill my cup with the desires
Of your will for my life
And your Kingdom;
In the sweet name
Of your son, Jesus.
AMEN!

PURPOSE BLUES

What is my purpose?
I'd like to know—
This journey started
42 years ago.
My direction unclear
My path a repeat;
Keep going nowhere
On a dead-end street...!?!?!

EMPTY PLEASURE

Once it's gone
It's gone
It comes with no future
It comes with no plan
It has no purpose
But acts on demand.
It brings
Plenty of selfishness
A mass of instant bliss
Inevitably leaves you alone
No chance to reminisce.
And all that's left
Is a faded dream...

IT'S MY CHOICE...

I have come to realize
That the one thing in life
I have control of is my choice(s)
YOU-have given us free will.
I can choose negativism and pessimism
Or to be positive and optimistic.
I can choose to love
Rather than hate
To have peace & joy
Rather than pain & sorrow.
To smile than to frown
To forgive than to hold
Bitterness in my heart
To have faith than to doubt
To move forward and grow
Or continue to keep my past alive
And allow it to cause my death.
Father, right now I choose
To give you control
Of all things in my life.
Help me to leave my struggles
At the cross and trust you!

HEARTBROKEN

Eight months ago
My heart was whole
And now it feels like one (hole).
Pieces keep crumbling
Pieces keep falling
Shreds can't keep it together;
Or keep the love
From floating away.

BREAK FREE!

Can we dry up
The cried tears
And replace them with flowers?
Can we untangle the words
And replace them with kindness?
Can we cancel the actions
And replace them with love?
YES, (what?) so to speak.
We can do this with wisdom,
With apologies, and forgiveness
By choosing to change
By casting out fear
And walking in God's love
For one another.
He made us fallible
But it takes only a little humility
And willing hearts
To break free from what keeps us
From His Will and moving forward.

GOD'S GRACE

Of all earthly achievements
Of all personal goals
God's GRACE is sufficient
To fill
Our empty souls.
His Grace is Awesome
As He!

MOVING FORWARD

In choosing to lose the past
To find your future
You realize this is the beginning
Of the end.

You struggle to maintain
A fighting strength
To overcome the madness

Though fear and courage
Consume you simultaneously
You are hopeful-
Much labor lies ahead
And your faith refuses to let go.

But this is a new day, Hallelujah!
Your desire to succeed
Holds a newer, richer perspective
YOU ARE DETERMINED!
This "you" is ME.

God says it's time for resolution
And reconciliation in our lives
Let's move forward.

AT THE CROSS

At the cross, at the cross
Is where my Lord and Savior
Embraced death and all sin
For my freedom and yours.

Let us not forget
The power of salvation
That was born
On the cross.

I WANT A MESSY MAN

M-mature
E-experienced
S-saved
S-stable
Y-young at heart

*Inspired while having a delicious salad at Jim & Nicks
with Kara in Smyrna, TN ☺

DREAM

Differentiate yourself from others
Recognize your passion
Empower your imagination
Act on desire
Make it happen...

AFFIRMATION FOR JESSICA & MELIA
(Or tween & teen girls in general)

My Precious Young Flower,
Your petals are so delicate
So fresh and oh, so tender.
Your youth is radiant
Your fruit is pure
Like drops of morning dew.
Please know that you are beautiful!
Be proud and in love with yourself!
Value your virtues...
So many want to be like you.

A LOVE NOTE FOR MY KIDS

(Nathan & Jessica Oliver)

YOU ARE MY DARLINGS
OH YES, YOU ARE
I LOVE YOU CLOSE AND
I LOVE YOU FAR
PLEASE KNOW MY LOVE IS SO TRUE
I'LL ALWAYS CHERISH YOU!

LOVE,
MOM

IT MAKES A DIFFERENCE

It would be nice to feel more appreciated
For you to truly know that I'm human
Not a high powered "super" machine
For you to know I have real feelings
And sometimes you hurt them---
Like when I sense your idea of what
I'm "supposed" to do or be.
Please don't take my servant hood out of context
Because of your selfishness, immaturity, and ignorance.
It makes a difference
That you know the depth of my love
Through my compassion for <u>you</u>
And my sacrifices for <u>you.</u>
It makes a difference
That I know you appreciate, love, and respect me
Simply because I am Mom.

THE INVITATION

You are invited
To a heart that is sincere,
A love that understands,
Is patient, and unselfish;
A mind that is pure
And has you on it.
To a world where you are respected,
Encouraged, and appreciated;
To a woman who loves,
Forgives, and refuses drama.
This invitation never expires
It's an ongoing event
Where joy and peace
Are greeters at the door;
Where HOPE is the orchestrator
No RSVP is required.
You are the only guest...
Let's leave the past behind,
Get ready for the time
Of your life!

CRYING OUT TO YOU!

Oh God, Oh God, how long?
I believe in You; the Creator,
I believe in your power,
But I get discouraged.
What have I done
That keeps me here?
Keeps me in bondage?
I desire to be obedient
So I pray.
I give and forgive.
I practice the golden rule,
and I maintain peace.
I love others even when
They don't love me back.
I go to church and worship You,
I listen and agree;
Teach my children
Your Truth and Your Word
And how to behave.
I walk Your way;
Seems I get left behind.
My progress looks like failure
Stuck in a cycle
Of hindrance and no gain.

I call out to You, Father!
'Cause I can't find my way!
You know my heart
But I can't see or
Feel you near me (at times).
I believe in Your son Jesus,
You said I can ask anything
In His Name and You
Will give it to me—
But You haven't
And I don't know why—
I'm just trying to live.
I'm not selfish
Or self righteous,
I try not to judge;
I'm human and Your child.
Please help me God!
I'm just trying to live.
I bleed for those like me and worse,
I ask for forgiveness
For times I've done things my way
Out of ignorance and fear.
I need relief
So the lion won't devour me.
Still, I give You all Praise
While crying out to You.

DON'T GO THERE

Let no emotions steal your joy
Not from within or elsewhere.
They are selfish and greedy.
The more you feed them
The more they grow
And thrive on each other's "feelings"
Until they have drained you
Of who you are; who you desire to be.
It's a short trip—
Soon the lies of the enemy
will deliver false messages
of the reflection of your beauty.
Just don't go there...
(My gift to Jessica. I love you, my Sweets)

SIMPLE RECIPE

By no means
Is he perfect
Neither am I,
But we accept
Each other
As we are.
I am free
To be me,
And he is
Who he is.
Together...
We make a recipe
For respect and peace.

MY MR. SUPER

My Mr. Super is 5'6" tall
And he is my personal hero.
He does not have super powers;
Does not wear a cape or spandex
But has great strength
In the WORD and promises of God.
My Mr. Super is very brave
But is not a public icon
Who flies in the big sky
With a secret identity
To save the day from evil.
No, My Mr. Super has no
Trait of fictional force
But he fears no one.
He fights enemies with prayer,
The good fight of faith
And authority given to him
By our Heavenly Father.
He is covered by the blood
Of our Lord and Savior, JESUS!
In whom he can do ALL things.
That makes him SUPER.

MOM'S ADVICE:

Set boundaries in your garden.
Even when the rain
Is mistreating you—
Be wise not to wither;
Your roots will be your strength
Reach for the Son!

ONLY ONE

You are desirable
By countless creatures of nature.
Few may pledge
To dance with you
In harmony.
Step carefully--
Only one
Will understand the music!

MY SON, NATHAN

You are the one
Who launched this test
Of motherhood for me—
At times I wasn't sure
If it was something
I should be.
But when you smile
I smile too—
And I feel proud
God gave me you.
You make me laugh
When I want to be tough;
Then I let go
Of the trivial stuff.
'Cause when you smile
I smile too—
I feel so proud
God gave me you.
I love you, my son!

A SILLY RHYME
(For My "Bugs")

With a warm hug
You make me feel
Like a bug in a rug
On top of a hill.
Where the clouds glide low
And a cool breeze blows
Soft, cuddly winds,
That tickle my toes.

FOR OUR CHILDREN AS THEY GROW

Continue being who you are
Follow TRUTH & LIGHT
And remember...
It's always a good time
To do what's right!

SHOW ME

Father, show me what you want me to do
Put your vision in my eyes so I can see
Your words in my ears to hear you clearly
Wisdom in my mouth before I speak
Renew my mind when I am weak
Direction in my walk so I don't fall
Love in my heart to conquer all
Lord, show me what you want me to do
I know trusting you will see me through!

CAN'T GIVE IT UP!

I didn't understand
No, not until
I heard the voice
Of my Father's Will
He gave me this gift
Before even the day
We came to earth
It was meant this way
I am his
And we are to be
He is mine
That makes us "we"
It was appointed
Long ago
It wasn't clear then
But now I know
Obedience is key
For my peace
You see
So I can't give up
That part of me.

STAND BY ME

You say I'm strong
I believe this is true
But there are some things
I still need from you.
It's just not enough to be
An overcomer, you see--
I need you "all in"
Standing by and with me.

I PERSEVERED...

When I was broken
When I was slandered
When I was deceived
When I was empty
When I failed
When I was betrayed
When I was alone
When I was controlled
When I was depressed
When I didn't fit in
When I was lost
When I was insecure
When I had no peace
When I was frustrated
When I didn't understand
When I needed hope
When I wasn't good enough
Nor even had enough;
Through God's Grace
I PERSEVERED!

GIFT OF MERCY

He gave me the gift of Mercy
That's why I can forgive
The offenses made against me
For His Love is why I live.
He gave me the gift of Mercy
To allow my wounds to heal
And exalt Himself in me
So all will know He's real!

MY GRANDBOY, Z

I never knew how sweeter life could be
You open a new kind of joy in me
My love for you is beyond surreal
You'll never know the emotions I feel
I miss your hugs, your laugh and smile
When I haven't seen you for a while
I never knew that you would be
The first and only (so far) to call me Gigi.

TOXIC STRUGGLE

We were so young
When we first wed
I wanted to defy
What naysayer said.
When the road got rough
Didn't want to give up-
So I stayed awhile
In the lies and denial
In your painful words
And sarcastic swords
Made excuses for you
Even though I knew-
That "we" were O-V-E-R!
I killed the poison in the struggle
So we both could live.

ABOUT THE AUTHOR

 Regina Johnson, an educator residing in North Alabama, debuts with Whispers of My Heart, a captivating blend of poetry, memoir, and personal history. With a passion for word expressions, Regina reflects on 26 years of life's trials, joys, and blessings. As a single mom, co-parent, and spiritual seeker, she weaves a tapestry of hope and inspiration. When not writing, Regina enjoys sewing and cherishing moments with her family.

Contact the author: Email: reginaj1633@gmail.com